Child Safe

A
Parent's Guide
to
First Aid
and
Safety

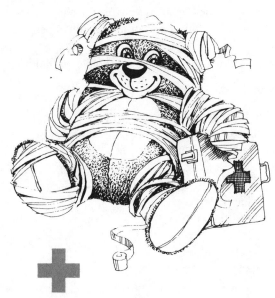

The Canadian Red Cross Society

StayWell

Printed in Canada
Composition by Jansom
Printing/binding by PrintCrafters Inc.

The StayWell Health Company Ltd.
780 Township Line Road
Yardley, PA 19067-4200

ISBN 1-58480-136-0
    04 05 / 10 9 8 7

The Basic Life Support skills outlined in this publication are consistent with the Guidelines 2000 for Cardiopulmonary Resuscitation and Emergency Cardiovascular Care.

Acknowledgements

The Canadian Red Cross Society wishes to express its sincere appreciation to the volunteers and staff who made this project possible. The growth and development of the ChildSafe program is the result of the work and dedication of many Red Cross Instructors from across the country. Their commitment to excellence made this training program and its resources possible.

A very special thank you to the volunteer members of the Society's Development Team who were responsible for this textbook: Karen Clark and Siegrid Goodrich.

Thank you also to Tim Sampson, the Vancouver Island Safety Council and The Canadian Cycling Association for their input and guidance.

Table of Contents

Safety

First Aid

Introduction

Caring for young children is a special responsibility. If you are a parent or someone who takes care of children, ChildSafe was developed for you.

The manual has two main sections, safety and first aid.

Safety

Many childhood injuries can be prevented if parents and care-givers behave safely and ensure that surroundings are safe. These sound safety habits can be taught to children. The safety section outlines three aspects of reducing injuries.

1. Examples of Safe Behaviour

Children learn by imitating others. Parents and care-givers are their main role models. Continual demonstration of safe behaviour can make it a natural part of children's lives.

2. Safe Surroundings

Children explore their world with an innocence that puts them at risk. Parents can use the many ideas in these sections to become more aware of possible dangers and to reduce risks.

3. Safety Education

Safety habits are learned. To be most effective, this education should be ongoing and geared to the age of the child. This section provides ideas for training children in safety.

Injuries are most likely to occur when:
- Children and parents are tired, usually before nap time, in the late afternoon or before bed;
- Children are overactive or rushed and aren't allowed enough time to do things carefully;
- Parents are ill and unable to supervise their children with their usual patience and care;
- Parents are under emotional stress and their attention is distracted;
- Daily routines are disrupted;
- People other than usual care-givers are supervising the children.

Baby Equipment

- Consumer and Corporate Affairs Canada issues safety guidelines that govern many products for children. Contact your local office for information.
- Although guidelines provide considerable protection, there is no substitute for your own careful inspection and judgement.

Cribs

Examples of Safe Behaviour
- Particular care is taken if purchasing used cribs as they may not conform to current safety standards. Large toys are not allowed in the crib. Children may use them as steps to climb over the edge.
- Children are never tied or harnessed into a crib. The cords may cause strangulation.
- Torn or punctured bumper pads are immediately replaced.
- Once children are able to climb out unaided or are taller than 90 cm (3'), they are graduated to a bed.
- Cribs are regularly checked for wear and tear and repaired immediately.

Safe Surroundings - Check It Out!
☐ No more than 6 cm (2³/₈") exists between the crib slats.
☐ Double locks are installed on the drop side of the crib.
☐ The crib is checked for cracks, sharp edges, loose or missing slats and missing hardware.
☐ The height from mattress support to the top rail is at least 66 cm (2'2") when the support is in its lowest position.
☐ The mattress is less than 15 cm (6") thick.
  When the mattress is pushed into one corner, there is no more than a 3 cm (1¼") gap between the mattress and the other end of the crib frame.

□ Soft mattresses are avoided; they can create "gap traps."

□ Cribs that have ornate headboards with a cut-out pattern are avoided as they may trap little arms, heads or clothing.

□ Corner posts extend no more than 3 cm (1¼") above the headboards.

□ When children become strong enough to pull themselves up on toys suspended across the crib, the toys are removed.

□ Mattress supports are tested by rattling the mattress and thumping it on the top and bottom. Collapsing supports can be extremely dangerous.

Playpens

Examples of Safe Behaviour
• Once children can climb out of the playpen, it is no longer used.
• Playpens are regularly checked for wear and tear and repaired immediately.

Safe Surroundings - Check It Out!
□ Holes in the mesh sides are small enough so that buttons cannot be caught. A 6.4 mm (¼") button should not fit in the holes.

□ Playpens with four wheels are avoided as they are too easily moved and tipped. Two wheels are safer.

□ Playpen walls are sturdy and at least 48 cm (1'7") high.

□ Hinges are designed and located to prevent pinching.

High Chairs

Examples of Safe Behaviour
• The safety strap is always used.
• Older children are prevented from climbing onto the chair, even when unoccupied.
• High chairs are checked regularly for wear and tear and are repaired immediately.

Safe Surroundings - Check It Out!
□ A chair with a wide, stable base is best.
□ The chair is equipped with a safety strap.
□ The chair is inspected for places where children's fingers might get trapped.

Baby Strollers

Examples of Safe Behaviour
- A safety strap is always used.
- Brakes and wheels are regularly checked.
- Only light parcels are loaded on the back to avoid upsetting the balance.

Safe Surroundings - Check It Out!
- ☐ The stroller is equipped with a safety strap.
- ☐ Sharp edges are avoided.
- ☐ The manufacturer's guidelines for height and weight are carefully followed.

Baby Walkers

This item is **not recommended.** Walkers are very dangerous and delay infant development. Infants have received severe head injuries caused by walkers tipping over or falling down stairs.

Pacifiers

Examples of Safe Behaviour
- The pacifier is checked regularly and discarded if there is any sign of deterioration, e.g. discolouration or hardening and cracking of the nipple.
- If children develop a yeast infection in the mouth, the pacifier is discarded and a new one used only after the infection has cleared.

Safe Surroundings - Check It Out!
- ☐ At time of purchase, the pacifier is packaged to ensure sterility.
- ☐ Before using, the pacifier is cleaned according to the manufacturer's guidelines.
- ☐ The pacifier's guard or shield is large and rigid to prevent the baby from sucking in and choking on the nipple.
- ☐ The pacifier does not have a cord.

Child Carriers for a Bicycle

Examples of Safe Behaviour
- As the added weight of children in a carrier affects steering, parents practise riding with a similar weight load before riding with a child.
- The child's weight does not exceed the manufacturer's recommended load.
- The safety strap is installed so that the child cannot release it.
- The child wears an approved, impact-absorbent helmet that fits properly.
- The seat is checked regularly for wear and tear and repaired immediately.

Safe Surroundings - Check It Out!
- ☐ The carrier seat has adequate foot protection.
- ☐ High back and side supports prevent children from swinging.
- ☐ The seat is well fastened to the frame of the bicycle.

Safety Gates

Examples of Safe Behaviour
- Even when a safety gate is in place, children are not left unattended.
- Placing a footstool or other home-made barrier in front of the stairs is not used as an alternative to a gate.

Safe Surroundings - Check It Out!
- ☐ Child gates, properly fitted, are installed wherever stairs are exposed.
- ☐ Gates are installed in strict accordance with the manufacturer's instructions.
- ☐ The gate is anchored securely in the doorway or passage. Models held in place by a pressure bar are installed with the bar located on the side away from the children.

Babysitters

- Since more injuries occur in the home than in any other location, babysitters should have first aid training and the maturity to handle an emergency.

The following are tips on choosing and orienting a babysitter:
- Choose babysitters who demonstrate knowledge of how to prevent injuries. They should have taken first aid training or a babysitting course that includes first aid. The Canadian Red Cross Society offers these types of courses.
- Orient a new babysitter to your home. Show the sitter the first aid supplies, this book with its emergency telephone numbers, the escape plan in case of fire and how to control heat, stove, lights and fuse box.
- Be clear about activities and areas that are off limits to children.
- Leave the telephone number where you will be and the number of a neighbour who could be of assistance in an emergency.
- After the children are put to bed, the sitter should check each of them once an hour. Make it clear that the babysitter should not sleep.
- The sitter should not be allowed to entertain friends. He or she is hired to do a job and should not be distracted.
- The telephone should not be used for personal calls. It is for emergency use only.
- The sitter should know what the child is doing at all times.
- If possible, avoid asking babysitters to give medicine. If you must, give them careful instructions.
- Babysitters should not smoke. Smoking is a fire and health hazard. Smoke may cause or worsen children's colds, flu, asthma and bronchitis.
- Babysitters should not be expected to do chores. Their concern is for the safety of the child.
- Check out your babysitters thoroughly. Make unscheduled visits home until you are sure you can trust them.

Bicycle Safety

Choosing a Safe Bike

Examples of Safe Behaviour
- A bike that the child will "grow into" is not recommended. It won't be well suited to present needs and can result in loss of control and falls.
- The child has an opportunity to test drive a potential purchase for fit and comfort.

Safe Surroundings - Check It Out!
☐ A safe bike is the proper size. The child is able to stand over the frame while standing flat-footed with both feet on the ground.
☐ A child is able to use the brakes on the bike safely. If the child's hands are too small to use hand brakes, coaster brakes (foot brakes) are recommended.
☐ Tires are fully inflated. Check tires for proper pressure.
☐ The brakes work properly and the child is able to operate them safely.
☐ The wheels are tightly secured and true (round). Shake the wheels to check that they are secure at the hubs.
☐ The chain is oiled and tight.
☐ Spokes are not loose, bent or broken.
☐ The "bounce test":
   The bike is bounced on the road while the adult listens for shakes and rattles. A safe bike is a quiet bike.
☐ The seat post and handlebars are securely attached.

Bike Maintenance

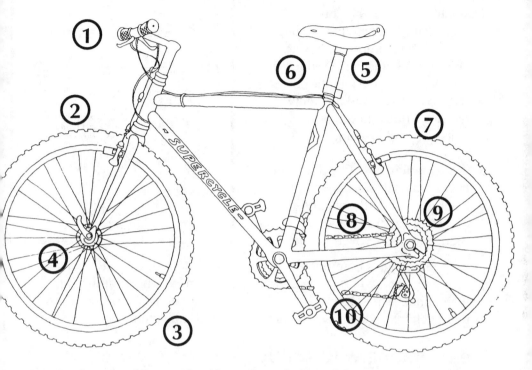

EVERY time you ride, you should run through this quick maintenance check list...

1. Squeeze the brake lever for adequate leverage.
2. Check the tire pressure. The ideal pressure is indicated on the side of the tire.
3. Bounce the bike and listen for rattles.
4. Check to make sure any quick release latches are secured.

AFTER an extended storage period, an extensive check-up is required. Follow steps 1 to 4, plus these 6 additional steps...

5. Wipe down the entire bike with a damp rag. Look for cracks in the frame, rim and cranks.
6. Check that bolts on the seat, seat post, handlebar stem and axles are tight.
7. Inflate the tires to the recommended pressure shown on the tire.
8. Check for loose, bent or broken spokes.
9. Derailleur levers should move easily when you shift, but not at all when you are not shifting. A screw or butterfly nut should allow you to adjust the lever movement.
10. Oil the chain and sprockets.

Choosing a Bicycle Helmet

Examples of Safe Behaviour

- Bicycle mishaps are the leading cause of head injuries for Canadian children. Helmets can reduce the number of bicycle fatalities by 80%.
- As a role model and for safety reasons, adults should always wear a helmet while cycling.

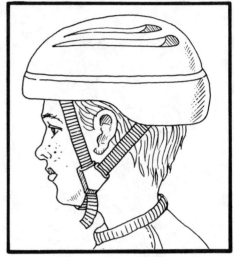

Safe Surroundings - Check It Out!

☐ Look for an ANSI (American National Standards Institute), Snell or CSA (Canadian Standards Association) approved helmet.

☐ A good helmet is comfortable for your child. The best way to make sure of the fit is to bring the child to the bike store when purchasing the helmet. The staff can help ensure that the helmet fits properly. A good helmet sits squarely on the head with a snug chin strap.

Co-operating with Traffic

Examples of Safe Behaviour

- Traffic Signals:
  Children should walk their bikes using the pedestrian crosswalks.
  REMEMBER: Even the safest cyclist must watch for drivers who aren't paying attention!
- Be Predictable:
  Good cyclists ride in a straight line when they go down the street. They don't swerve between parked cars or onto driveways. Good cyclists always look and signal before turning. A cyclist who is full of surprises often gets into trouble.
- Be Visible:
  Wear bright clothes (white and yellow are the brightest) even during the day. When motorists can see a cyclist, it's easier for them to cooperate with the cyclist.
  Young children should avoid riding after dark.

Safety Education

Bicycle Handling Skills

Before a child goes on the road with a bicycle, the skills necessary for the safe control of the bicycle are developed. The best place to practise these exercises is in a quiet parking lot or school courtyard.

- Balancing Exercises:
  Practise riding along the straight lines painted on the surface of the courtyard. Try this at slow and quick speeds, staying as close to the line as possible.
- Turning Exercises:
  Step 1. Is it safe to turn?
  The first step involved in making a turn in traffic is to make sure that it is safe to do so. Looking ahead, side to side AND behind you before turning is important. The SHOULDER CHECK is a necessary skill to develop. Have the child practice riding along the courtyard lines while shoulder checking. Encourage him to stay as close to the line as he can while shoulder checking.
  Step 2. Signalling a turn
  Review the hand signals with your child, allowing practise time while riding in the courtyard. The ability to ride with one hand without losing control is necessary for signalling.
- Stopping/Braking Exercises:
  Have the child practise stopping as close as possible to a line or "soft" obstacle without skidding or hitting it. Practise this at different speeds.
  Hand Brakes
      Both brakes must be used to make a safe, quick stop.
  Coaster Brakes (Foot Brakes)
      If these brakes are slammed on too quickly, skidding can result.

Rules of the Road

- A cyclist has the same rights and responsibilities as the driver of a car. This means that cyclists must follow all the rules of the road.

Riding with your Child

- Spend time riding with your child. When you ride together, stay behind your child in order to watch what he or she is doing and offer encouragement. As a role model, you will be able to demonstrate and reinforce good riding habits.

With thanks to Tim Sampson, the Vancouver Island Safety Council, B.C. and the Canadian Cycling Association.

Car Safety

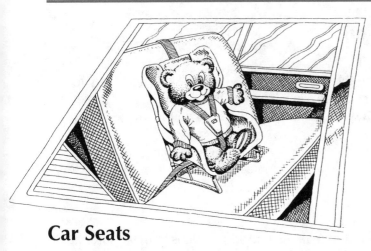

- Motor vehicle injuries are the number one cause of death of children in Canada.
- Never leave an infant or child alone in a car, even for a short time.

Car Seats

Examples of Safe Behaviour

- Approved infant and child car seats are essential safety equipment and are always used.
- For extra protection, the child rides only in the back seat. The most protected area is the centre.
- The child's comfort is important. A car seat is tested by placing the child in it and making sure that his or her arms can move freely once the harness is in place.
- If a car seat is purchased, ensure that it meets federal safety standards and check carefully for damage. Materials deteriorate over time. New car seats (or those less than 10 years old) are used.

Safe Surroundings – Check It Out!

☐ The seat is installed exactly as outlined in the manufacturer's instructions.

☐ The seat is pushed well down into the upholstery before being secured with the seat restraint.

☐ **Infant Seats** are used for infants weighing less than 10 kg (22 lbs.).

☐ **Child Seats** are used for children weighing 10 to 18 kg (22 to 40 lbs.).

☐ **Booster Seats** can be used for children weighing 18 to 27 kg (40 to 60 lbs.).

☐ **Seat Belts** are used for children who reach the weight limit (27 kg or 60 lbs.) and the height limit of the booster seat. The child is shown how to wear the belt so that it fits snugly over the upper thighs and the shoulder belt fits between the child's neck and arm.

☐ Vehicles are maintained in good working condition and drivers adhere to all safety rules.

Safety Education

Passenger safety rules for children:

- Always exit the car on the curb side.
- Remain seated and restrained while the car is moving.
- Do not distract the driver.
- Keep heads, arms and feet in the car.
- Controls are for the driver only, even when the car is parked.
- Ensure that everyone's fingers, hands and feet are clear before closing doors.
- Keep buckled up until the car is parked.

The reasons for these rules are discussed with your child.

Seat restraints are used by all passengers at all times.

Children are taught never to play near parked cars, e.g. driveways or parking lots.

Home Safety

- More injuries requiring medical attention occur in the home than in any other place.
- Special supervision is needed when visiting.

Reducing the Risk of Falls

Examples of Safe Behaviour
- Babies are constantly supervised when they are being bathed or changed.
- Crib sides are up and secure before the adult leaves the room.
- Infants are constantly supervised when in a high chair, stroller, grocery cart or baby carrier. These are equipped with a seat belt that is used at all times.
- Stairs are kept uncluttered, especially of toys.
- Toys are collected and stored periodically during the day.

Safe Surroundings - Check It Out!
- ☐ Child gates, properly fitted, are installed wherever stairs are exposed. Placing a footstool or other home made barrier in front of the stairs is not a safe alternative.
- ☐ Windows and balcony doors have child-proof latches.
- ☐ Balconies have protective barriers to prevent children from slipping through the bars. When children are on a balcony, they are constantly supervised.
- ☐ All carpets are anchored.

Reducing the Risk of Suffocation and Choking

Examples of Safe Behaviour
- All dry cleaning plastic covers and protective plastic covers on new products are tied in knots before disposal.
- Plastic bags are stored on a high shelf.
- Balloons are kept out of cribs or playpens to prevent suffocation from small pieces of a burst balloon.
- All family members sit quietly while eating food or candy.
- Children do not use pen tops as toys. They are easily swallowed and can obstruct breathing.
- Food is cut into "child-size" pieces.
- Latches are removed from old freezers and refrigerators.
- Pillows are not used for infants.

Reducing the Risk of Poisoning

Examples of Safe Behaviour
- Parents are careful with everyday medicines. The most common poison among children is non-prescription medication.
- Pharmacists are asked to put prescriptions in containers with safety lids.
- Parents take medicine in private because children mirror adult behaviour.
- The medicine cabinet is periodically cleared of old or unused portions of prescriptions. Containers are rinsed before disposal.
- After a party, ashtrays and unfinished drinks are immediately emptied. Tobacco and alcohol can be harmful to children.
- Food containers such as pop bottles are never used to store poisonous products.
- Hazardous goods are promptly disposed of. For information about safe disposal, contact your local municipal government.
- The local Poison Control Centre is contacted for a list of common household poisons.

Safe Surroundings - Check it Out!
☐ A protection area is established in each room for all poisons. After **each** use of a poisonous product, it is returned to the shelf or to a locked closet.
☐ House plants are kept away from children who may decide to taste them. A number of household and outdoor plants are poisonous.
☐ Medicine is kept in a locked storage place that is beyond reach and climbing access.

Warning Symbols - When any of these symbols appear on a container, the contents are dangerous and must be stored appropriately.

| Poison | Flammable | Explosive | Corrosive |

Reducing the Risk of Fire and Burns

Examples of Safe Behaviour
• Your fire department may be contacted for information on inspecting your home for fire hazards and reviewing your fire escape plan.
• Bedroom doors are closed when the family is sleeping. Doors are important barriers to fire.
• Flammable liquids and materials such as solvent-soaked cloths are stored in approved, sealed containers.
• Cooking areas are kept free from clutter to avoid igniting pot holders, aprons and other kitchen items.
• Saucepan handles are pointed toward the back of the stove to prevent children from grabbing them.
• Coffee and tea cups and pots are kept out of children's reach.
• After parties ash trays, furniture and cushions are checked for burning cigarettes.
• Smoking is not allowed in bed or lying down.
• Matches are stored away from the reach and sight of children.

Safe Surroundings - Check It Out!

☐ All switches on the electrical panel are clearly labelled. To ensure easy access in an emergency, items are not stored in front of the panel.

☐ Covers are placed on all unused electrical outlets.

☐ Multiple-cord or octopus plugs are not used since they may over-heat.

☐ Loose cords are secured out of the way.

☐ Approved smoke detectors are installed in the hallway near the sleeping area, at the top of the stairs and in every bedroom. These are tested regularly according to manufacturer's recommendations.

☐ Flammable liquids are stored in their original sealed containers outside the house.

☐ An approved all-purpose chemical fire extinguisher is kept in the kitchen.

☐ If there are fuses in the electrical panel, only appropriately-sized fuses are used. Spare fuses are kept on hand. Pennies and metal foil are never used.

☐ Space heaters are placed out of the reach of children.

☐ Garbage and material for recycling are stored neatly and disposed of frequently.

Family Fire Escape Plan for a House

Draw a floor plan of your home. Mark the normal exit from each room and an emergency exit, such as a window, that can be used if fire blocks the doorway.

Designate a location where everyone will meet if the family must escape from a fire. Practise the family fire drill once a year.

What to do in a house fire:

• When you hear the smoke alarm, roll out of bed onto the floor. Shout "fire" and get out.

• Crawl to the door and touch it. If it is warm, do not open it. Escape via the emergency exit.

• If the door is cool, open it cautiously and crawl down the hall to the nearest exit. Be sure to practice this with your children.

• Join the rest of the family at the special meeting spot.

- After everyone is together, go to a neighbour's home to call the Fire Department.
- Meet the fire trucks and tell the firefighters that everyone is out of your house.

Family Fire Escape Plan for an Apartment

Draw a floor plan of the building. Map out two emergency exit routes. An elevator is **not** a suitable exit route.

Practise the family fire drill once a year. Walk the escape routes.

What to do in an apartment fire:
- When you hear the alarm, feel the door to the hall. If it is warm, do not open it. Unlock the door so that firefighters can open it.
- Seal off any cracks with wet towels. Block vents to prevent smoke from entering the apartment.
- Take refuge in a room with a window. Open it for ventilation. Hang out a sheet to signal for help and wait for rescue.
- If the door to the hall is cool, open it cautiously. Brace yourself to slam it shut if there is pressure against the door, or if the hall is filled with smoke.
- If the way is clear, close the door behind you without locking it. Proceed to the nearest emergency exit. Close the exit door behind you; doors slow down fires. Leave the building.

Fire: If children spot a fire, they should know to shout "fire," get out of the building as quickly as possible and run to a spot where everyone in the family has agreed to meet. **Shout and Get Out.**

Safety Education

A few clear, simple rules that are consistently enforced work best. Rules also apply to visiting children.

Playground Safety

- Playgrounds are the site of many serious injuries.
- The majority of playground injuries are caused by falls.

Neighbourhood Playgrounds

Examples of Safe Behaviour
- Playgrounds at home, in parks and at schools all require adult supervision. Equipment is designed to develop physical skills and children often use it in imaginative and dangerous ways.

Safe Surroundings - Check It Out!
- Some public playgrounds are unsafe. Parents should examine park and school playgrounds for safety hazards. The most serious injuries result from falls onto hard surfaces. Preferred surfaces include loose sand, pine bark and pea gravel 25 to 30 cm (10" to 12") deep. Your local community centre, parks board or school board office can be called if you see unsafe or broken equipment in a public park.

Backyard Playground Equipment

Examples of Safe Behaviour
- When selecting playground equipment, user age and size is considered.
- All equipment is installed and maintained according to the manufacturer's specifications.
- All equipment is thoroughly and regularly checked using the following guide and any checklist provided by the manufacturer.

Safe Surroundings - Check It Out!

☐ Moving parts are covered to protect fingers and toes.

☐ Rings are less than 20 cm (8") in diameter, so that a child's head cannot fit through.

☐ Swing seats are made of soft material such as canvas or rubber. An old tire and rope is often a safe and inexpensive alternative.

☐ Climbing equipment can be easily descended.

☐ Components allow for the grip of a five-year-old, 4 cm (1⅝") in width.

☐ Slides have an incline less than 30 degrees. The ideal slide length is twice the height of the slide.

☐ Side rails are installed for slides over 120 cm (4').

☐ The slide exit is parallel to the ground and 30 to 40 cm (12" to 16") high.

☐ Steps and rungs are 18 to 28 cm (7" to 11") apart.

☐ Sand boxes are fitted with a cover to keep dogs and cats from excreting in the sand.

☐ Unleaded paint is used for playground equipment.

Check These Out Every Two Weeks...

☐ Bolts, screws and other sharp edges are taped. Duct, carpet or electrical tape will work.

☐ All nuts and clamps are tight.

☐ "S" hooks and other hangers are closed.

☐ Worn ropes and rusted chains are replaced.

☐ All moving metal parts are oiled as needed.

☐ Wooden equipment is sanded to remove rough areas.

☐ Slide landing pits are regularly refilled, levelled and cleaned.

☐ Anchoring is checked and supports re-buried if protruding.

Safety Education

• Children are shown how to use equipment properly. Any dangerous behaviour is immediately stopped.

• A few simple rules aimed at preventing serious injury are made and enforced.

• Rules apply to all children, including visitors.

Toy Safety

- Even the most harmless-looking toy can become dangerous.
- The Canadian Toy Testing Council issues a list of guidelines for choosing toys.

Examples of Safe Behaviour
- Toys are selected according to each child's age and ability, using the manufacturer's suggested age level and your own judgement.
- Younger children who may have access to the toy are also kept in mind.
- All instructions are carefully read and followed.
- All packaging material is removed and safely discarded.
- Toys are inspected regularly for damage. If the toy is damaged, it is repaired or discarded.
- Sharp edges are avoided.
- Damaged rattles are discarded.
- Batteries are checked regularly. Used batteries, which can leak corrosive liquid, are appropriately discarded.
- Extra care is needed when choosing toys for infants.

Safe Surroundings - Check It Out!
INFANTS
- ☐ Rattles and teethers are made of durable, smooth materials. Labels are checked to ensure the materials are non-toxic.
- ☐ Toys are completely washable.
- ☐ Brittle plastic toys, which can be dangerous if broken, are avoided.
- ☐ Toys and detachable pieces are not small enough to fit in the mouth, eyes, ears or nose.
- ☐ Toys with strings are never given to infants because of the risk of strangulation.
- ☐ Protective knobs top the shaft-like handles of pull and push toys.
- ☐ The paint on toys is non-toxic.

- ☐ Seams on plush toys are well sewn and sturdy. Eyes, nose, hair and buttons are attached firmly and checked regularly. Painted or embroidered facial features are safer.
- ☐ Squeakers and other noise mechanisms in squeeze toys are firmly imbedded.
- ☐ Mobiles are fastened securely and well out of the reach of infants.

Safe Surroundings - Check It Out!
CHILDREN
- ☐ Wooden toys are glued or screwed together, not nailed, ensuring that all edges are smooth.
- ☐ Paints, crayons, markers and finger paints are non-toxic and washable.
- ☐ Wheels on toy cars and trucks cannot be removed to expose sharp pieces of metal.
- ☐ All metal edges are rounded or smooth.
- ☐ Ride-around toys are well balanced and selected according to the size of the child.
- ☐ "Toy" head gear is never used. Regulation baseball, hockey, skateboarding and bicycle helmets will serve the child better.
- ☐ Electrical toys bear the Canadian Standards Association (CSA) label to confirm that they have been tested.
- ☐ Costumes are made of flame retardant materials. Face masks are avoided. Face paints are safe because they do not block vision. They are also fun to use.
- ☐ Large toy boxes and other containers have air holes in case children decide to hide inside. Tightly fitting lids and doors with latches are avoided.
- ☐ Toy boxes without tops avoid the risk of slamming lids catching little fingers.

Safety Education

- The child is shown how the toy may be used.
- Some toys for older children are hazardous to infants. Older children are taught to keep these toys away from younger ones.
- A box or special place for toy storage is assigned. Children are shown where toys are kept when not in use.
- Children are kept away from purses, which are stored in a closet or on a counter top, out of reach.

Water Safety

- Two-thirds of children who drown are non-swimmers. They are especially at risk in unsupervised areas such as ponds, creeks, wells and excavations.

Backyard Pools and Hot Tubs

Examples of Safe Behaviour
- Children are constantly supervised when playing in or around a pool or hot tub.
- Hot tubs are securely covered and locked when not in use.
- Decks around the pool or hot tub are kept clean and clear of debris; slippery surfaces can cause injuries.
- Close attention is paid to the surface of the diving board; make sure that the slip-resistant surface is always in good repair.
- All cups and dishes used at pool side are non-breakable.
- Electrical appliances are never allowed near the pool.
- All floating toys are removed when pool time is over.

Safe Surroundings - Check It Out!
- ☐ Basic lifesaving equipment is available at all times, including a lightweight, strong pole with blunt ends or a ring buoy with a long throwing rope. Your local Health Act outlines pool safety equipment requirements.
- ☐ A lifeline across the pool where the deep end slope begins will separate the deep from the shallow end and may help keep inexperienced swimmers out of deep water.
- ☐ Electrical equipment used to operate the pool or hot tub conforms to electrical code requirements.
- ☐ A phone is installed on the pool deck with a list of emergency numbers posted beside it.

☐ An outdoor pool is protected by a fence, wall, building or enclosure which children cannot get through or over. Your local municipality will have fencing requirements for your area. Many communities require a barrier that will not allow any external handhold. Gates should have self-closing latches above the reach of toddlers and hardware for permanent locking.
☐ All pool chemicals are stored in a secure area.

Bath Tubs

Examples of Safe Behaviour
• An infant is never left alone in a tub, even for a few seconds, while the parent answers the door or phone. Drownings can occur in even a few centimetres of water.
• All pre-school children are closely supervised. School- aged children are supervised until they demonstrate consistent safe behaviour.
• Babysitters or older siblings are not expected to bathe infants.
• Bath temperature is checked by splashing water on the inner wrist or elbow before the infant or child is placed in the bath.

Safe Surroundings - Check It Out!
☐ Water taps are tightly turned off to prevent a child from accidentally turning on the hot water.
☐ If faucets have sharp edges, protective covers are purchased.

Neighbourhoods

Safe Surroundings - Check It Out!
☐ Wells, excavations, ponds and creeks on your property are fenced or covered.
☐ Protective fences and coverings are requested in hazardous areas which you do not own.

The Beach

Examples of Safe Behaviour
- Children are never allowed to play near water without close supervision. Lifeguards are not a substitute for parental supervision. Children are watched constantly; drowning can occur in seconds.
- Inflatable arm supports are not recommended. They give both children and parents a false sense of security and do not prevent drowning. They also interfere with the process of learning to swim.
- Inflatable toys can easily deflate or pop and will no longer support a child. They should be used only under close adult supervision.

Safe Surroundings - Check It Out!
The swimming area is checked for hazards such as:
- ☐ drop offs
- ☐ deep water
- ☐ shallow water (dangerous to dive)
- ☐ weeds
- ☐ submerged rocks, fences or other debris
- ☐ currents (river and tidal)
- ☐ undertow
- ☐ heavy surf
- ☐ heavy boat traffic.

Boating

Examples of Safe Behaviour
- Proper use of your boat and its safety equipment is learned before going out.
- Weather conditions and forecasts are checked before departing. A "float plan" is filed by advising family, friends, or marina officials where you are going and when you plan to return, making sure that you let them know when you return.
- Children and adults wear personal flotation devices (PFDs) or lifejackets whenever on deck and safety lines are used when needed.

Safe Surroundings - Check It Out!

☐ At least one approved lifejacket or approved personal flotation device (PFD) is on board for each person.

☐ A PFD is an alternative to a lifejacket. Children use PFDs fitted with a crotch strap. Both PFDs and lifejackets are carefully chosen to match the wearer's size and weight. Approved devices say "DOT (Department of Transport) Approved" or "MOT (Ministry of Transport) Approved". Lifejackets or PFDs are worn by everyone who is boating **at all times.**

☐ All pleasure craft, power vessels, sailing vessels, canoes, kayaks and rowboats carry safety equipment in good working order. To find out exactly what is needed for your boat, check the **Safe Boating Guide** from the Canadian Coast Guard.

Safety Education

SWIMMING

• Children are warned of the dangers of playing near or swimming in unsupervised bodies of water.

• Children never enter the water without permission from and supervision by a competent adult with water safety training. Non-swimmers stay in the shallow end of the pool or swimming area.

• Sensible safety rules are established at the very beginning and enforced consistently and firmly. The **reasons** for each rule are reviewed with the children. Basic safety rules are displayed on a sign at the poolside to inform visitors.

• Swim with a buddy. Sudden cramps can sink the most accomplished swimmer.

• Swim in good weather, during daylight.

• Non-swimmers do not use inner tubes or air mattresses in the water.

• Inflatable toys that have floated away are not chased. They can draw the pursuer too far from shore.

• When distance swimming at the beach, it is safest to swim parallel to shore.

• Before diving or sliding headfirst into unknown water, the shape of the pool bottom and the water depth is checked. At least 8 meters (25 feet) of clear water is needed before diving. Diving is not allowed in above ground pools.

- One person at a time is allowed on diving boards.
- Swimmers stay away from underneath diving boards while playing.
- One person at a time is allowed on slides. Sliding is safest sitting down, feet first.

Learning to swim is a progression of small steps. First, children learn to get into the water, then to put their faces in and later to open their eyes under water. Parents play a large part in this progression. Initial experiences in the water are shared with parents.

Many pools across Canada offer the Canadian Red Cross Swimming and Water Safety Program. When swimming with children, reinforce the safety concepts taught during the lessons.

BOATING
- Adults can set a good example by wearing their Personal Flotation Devices and by following safety rules.
- Small craft can be unstable. Children are taught to stay low in the boat. If changing positions is necessary, one person moves at a time, keeping low.
- Children are taught how to use a boat radio and fire extinguisher in case of an emergency.
- Older children are taught to take an increasing responsibility for family boat safety. They are involved in filing the float plan, checking safety equipment and weather and loading the boat in a balanced way.
- Survival techniques, such as climbing onto an overturned boat and huddling together in the water, are practised and discussed regularly.

SKATING AND ICE TRAVEL

The following safety rules provide a good basis for children:

- Ice must be a minimum of 15 cm (6") thick before it can support people.
- Skate with a buddy.
- When walking across unknown ice, carry a pole or hockey stick parallel to the ice surface.

If you fall through the ice:

- In shallow water, feel for the bottom with your feet and break ice towards shore until you can slide up onto thicker ice.
- In deep water, flutter kick your feet and extend your hands forward along the ice until you can slide up onto it. Roll over. Slowly crawl to safety.
- After getting out of danger, get to shelter and change into warm clothing to prevent hypothermia.

First Aid

This simple and easy-to-use first aid guide will assist you in dealing with injured children.

It is important to remember that it may be very traumatic to do first aid on children. Some people calmly perform first aid on other people's children but, faced with their own injured child, freeze or panic. If this happens to you, take a couple of deep breaths, tell yourself that you **can** help and begin some of the first aid steps that are outlined in this manual. Although you may feel upset, acting calmly will help the situation.

Please note that this manual alone is not a substitute for training from a qualified Red Cross ChildSafe Instructor.

Primary First Aid Sequence

CHECK FOR DANGER
- First to yourself
- Then to the casualty

CHECK LEVEL OF CONSCIOUSNESS
- Conscious: Responsive and alert
- Unconscious: Unresponsive

CALL FOR HELP
- Send someone to call for the Emergency Medical Services (EMS).
- If alone, "CALL FIRST."
- Ask someone for assistance.

CARE FOR:
- Airway
    Open using head tilt, chin lift.
- Breathing
    Look-listen-feel for no more than 10 seconds.
- Circulation
    Check for signs of circulation for no more than 10 seconds.
    Check for movement, coughing, effective breathing, and
    appropriate colour of skin. Feel for a pulse.
      Infant: brachial pulse (upper arm)
      Child: carotid pulse (neck)
- Deadly bleeding
    Search from head to toe.

COVER THE CHILD AND CARE FOR OTHER INJURIES

The Emergency Medical System

As a bystander trained in first aid, you are the first link in the **EMERGENCY MEDICAL SYSTEM (EMS)**. The system is designed to get emergency assistance to injured or ill people and to transport them to hospital. The EMS system varies from community to community. Many areas have a "9-1-1" system, while others use a local number.

When to Call for Help

As a general rule, call the ambulance for any of the following conditions:
- unconsciousness or altered level of consciousness
- breathing problems: difficulty breathing or no breathing
- no signs of circulation
- severe bleeding
- vomiting blood or passing blood
- poisoning
- convulsions, severe headache or slurred speech
- injuries to head, neck or back
- possible broken bones
- persistent chest pain or pressure

Always call the Emergency Medical System if the situation involves:
- fire or explosion
- poisonous gas
- downed electrical wires
- swift-moving water
- motor vehicle collisions
- a casualty who cannot be moved easily.

In other cases, trust your instincts. Call if you are unsure.

How to Call the Emergency Medical System (EMS)

Your local emergency number will be answered by a dispatcher in a communication centre. Based on the information provided, a decision is made as to what resources (i.e. police, ambulance or fire) to send.

Make sure that the emergency numbers for your area and your address are posted near every phone in your home.

Most dispatchers will ask for the following information:
- specific location of the emergency
- telephone number from which the call is being made
- caller's name
- how many people are involved
- condition of the patient
- what is being done for the patient

If you are providing the first aid, it is best to send someone else to make the call. Tell them to "hang up last," ensuring that the dispatcher has all the necessary information.

If you are alone and the casualty is unresponsive, shout for help. If no one else can call EMS, you must call yourself.

Allergies

Definition

◆ An allergic reaction occurs when something that a child is sensitive to is introduced to the body. Although almost any substance may trigger a reaction, the most common are peanuts, nuts, eggs, shellfish, medications and insect stings.

Severe Reactions

What to look for:

- tightness of throat
- breathing difficulty
- generalized itching
- blotches on skin
- raised, reddish-pink swelling
- anxiety, weakness
- shock
- abdominal cramps
- diarrhoea or vomiting
- unconsciousness

CAUTION: Although most allergic reactions are not serious, on occasion they can become life-threatening. Watch closely for any signs of breathing difficulty.

What to do:

1. Call the ambulance.
2. Keep the child calm and restrict movement.
3. If the child has an "ana kit," help him use it.

4. Carefully watch the airway and breathing for any signs of difficulty. See **Breathing/CPR**, page 47.

Bites and Stings
Bees and Wasps

What to look for:

- itching and pain in the affected area
- swelling in the affected area

What to do:

1. Find out if the child is known to be sensitive to stings. If he has an "ana kit," help him use it.

2. Rinse the affected area. Remove the stinger by gently scraping it out. Do not use tweezers as squeezing the stinger may inject more poison.

3. Apply a cold compress to the bite area to control swelling for 15 minutes per hour. Calamine or another lotion may be used to relieve the itching.

CAUTION: Most insect bites, although painful and uncomfortable, are harmless. However, if a child shows signs of airway or breathing difficulty, call an ambulance immediately. See **Breathing/CPR**, page 47.

3.

Bites and Stings
Ticks and Leeches

Ticks
What to do:
1. Remove the tick with tweezers, grasping it as close to the skin as possible and pulling *slowly*. If you do not have tweezers, use a glove, plastic wrap, or a piece of paper to protect your fingers.
2. Wash your hands immediately.
3. Do not try to burn a tick off, do not coat it with petroleum jelly or nail polish, and do not prick it with a pin. If you cannot remove the tick or if its mouthparts stay in the skin, see a doctor.
4. When the tick is out, wash the area with soap and water. Use an antiseptic or antibiotic ointment to prevent infection. If a rash or flu-like symptoms occur later, seek medical help.

NOTE:
Children should be checked frequently and thoroughly for ticks after outdoor activities where ticks are present.

Leeches (Blood Suckers)
What to do:
1. Sprinkle with salt, then remove. Wash the wound area with soap and water.
2. Watch for signs of infection, redness, swelling and pain at the injury site.

Bites and Stings
Human and Animal

What to do:

1. If the bite wound is **bleeding severely,** apply direct pressure with a clean cloth, elevate the limb and seek medical attention.

2. If the bite wound is **not bleeding severely,** wash with a mild soap and water. Do not apply antiseptics, lotions or creams.

   Cover the wound with a sterile dressing and bandage the dressing in place. Seek medical attention.

3. Comfort the child. Keep him warm.

NOTE:

Have someone note the location of the animal so it can be captured for examination.

Human bites can easily become infected (page 83).

Bites and Stings
Snake Bite

What to do:

1. Keep the child quiet and still.

2. Seek medical attention immediately. If possible, carry the child. Walking increases the circulation of the poison.

3. Lower the bite area below the child's heart to stop the absorption of snake venom.

4. For a bite on an arm or leg, do not apply a tourniquet. If a child cannot get advanced medical care within 30 minutes, you may apply a **constricting band** to slow the flow of venom throughout the body.

5. Watch for breathing problems. If the child stops breathing, turn to **Breathing/CPR**, page 47.

6. Comfort the child. Keep him warm.

CAUTION: Although death from snake bite is rare, medical attention should always be sought. Children, because of their small body size, are at greater risk than adults.

NOTE:
It is very helpful if the snake can be identified so that the correct antitoxin can be used. If you cannot identify it, take careful note of its markings.

Bleeding
Cuts and Wounds

What to do:

1. Apply direct pressure to the cut with a clean cloth. If nothing clean is available, use your hand with the fingers flat.

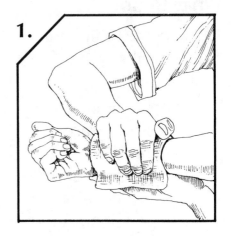

2. Have the child sit or lie down and keep still.

   Elevate a bleeding limb higher than the heart unless you suspect a broken bone.

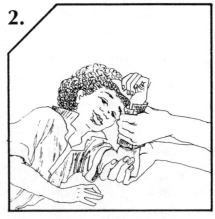

3. For severe bleeding, shout for help. Send someone to call an ambulance immediately.

4. If the cloth soaks through, **do not remove it**. Apply another cloth on top.

5. Tie the cloth in place with a bandage. Never tie a bandage around the neck; use tape.

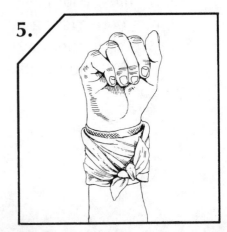

After the bleeding has stopped:

6. Use a sling or bandages to immobilize the injured limb if transporting the child is necessary.

7. Check circulation frequently. If the area below the wound is cold or blue compared to the other limb, the bandage is too tight.

8. Comfort the child. Keep him warm.

9. Seek medical attention.

☞ Red Cross Memory Aid:
    R = rest
    E = elevation
    D = direct pressure

Bleeding
Impaled Object

What to do:

1. Expose the wound.
2. Stabilize the object and control bleeding by applying dressings around it.
3. Hold the dressings in place with bandages.
4. Seek medical attention immediately.
5. Comfort the child. Keep her warm.

NOTE:

Ask your doctor if inoculations are necessary.

CAUTION: Do not remove an impaled object - severe bleeding and increased damage may result.

Bleeding
Internal Bleeding

What to look for:

- history of a severe blow to the chest, back or abdomen
- severe thirst
- pain over the injured area
- air hunger (yawning or gasping)
- feeling of faintness
- vomit that is dark red in colour
- coughing up blood
- swelling

CAUTION: Do not elevate the child's feet. Do not give the child anything to drink. Do not move a child who may have a head or neck injury unless breathing is a problem.

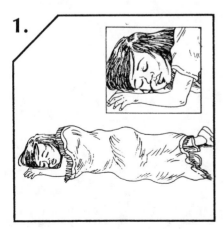

What to do:

1. If the child has difficulty breathing because of bleeding from the nose, mouth or ears, place the child in the recovery position.
2. Send someone to call an ambulance.
3. Comfort the child. Keep her warm.

Bleeding
Nosebleeds

What to do:

1. Have the child sit down.
2. Tilt the child's head forward slightly.
3. Pinch the nose firmly, just below the bone.
4. Hold firmly for 10 full minutes.
5. If bleeding continues, seek medical attention.

3.

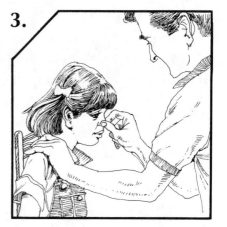

NOTE:

Cold compresses on the forehead and/or back of the neck may help to slow bleeding.

Bleeding
Scrapes

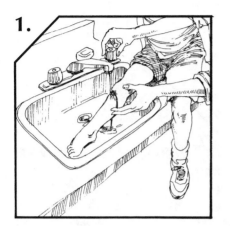

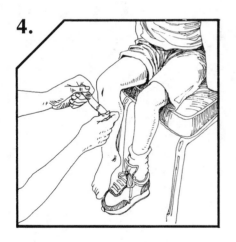

What to do:

1. Clean the scraped area by rinsing it with running water.
2. Gently wash the area around the wound with mild soap and water.
3. Blot dry with a sterile gauze dressing.
4. Cover with a sterile non-stick dressing.

NOTE:

Seek medical attention if the scrape is over a large area or if it becomes infected. If infected, there will be an increase in redness, swelling and pain.

Blisters

What to do:

1. Do not break a blister. The body is protecting a damaged area by creating a blister.

2. Place a large, loose bandage over the blister to prevent the child from breaking it.

2.

3. If the blister has broken, gently wash it with mild soap and water. Cover the area with a sterile dressing and bandage.

NOTE:

For large blisters or a large area of the body with blisters, seek medical attention.

Breathing/CPR
Infant Under 1 Year

If the infant does not respond to tapping or shouting,

Rescue Breathing Infant

1. Shout for help and send someone to call EMS. If you are alone, "CALL FIRST."

2. Tilt the head to open the airway by placing your hand on the infant's forehead. With your other hand, lift the infant's chin, keeping clear of the throat.

3. Check breathing for no more than 10 seconds. Place your cheek near the infant's nose and mouth. Listen and feel for air. Look for movement of the chest.

4. If the infant is breathing, care for **Unconsciousness**, page 95.

CAUTION: Do not tilt the head if you suspect a back or neck injury. Gently lift the lower jaw forward without moving the neck. Tilt the head only if you cannot inflate the chest.

CAUTION: Because an infant's lung capacity is so small, use only the air you can hold in your cheeks.

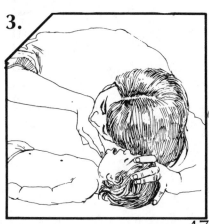

47

5.

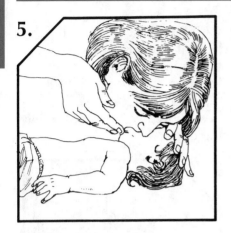

CAUTION: If the infant vomits, roll him on his side, clean out the mouth and resume Rescue Breathing.

5. If the infant is **not breathing**, seal your mouth over the infant's mouth and nose. Attempt to gently deliver two small, slow puffs. Look for movement of the chest.

6. If the chest has not moved after the first breath, try blowing in again, making sure that the head is tilted correctly (see step 2).

If the chest still does not move, turn to **Choking**, **Infant**, page 61.

7. If air has entered, **check for signs of circulation**. Look for movement, coughing, breathing, and appropriate colour of skin. Place two fingers close to the bone inside the infant's upper arm. Feel for a brachial pulse for no more than 10 seconds.

7.

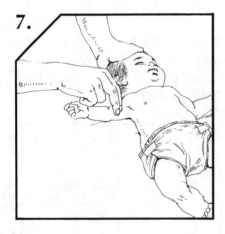

8. **IF** the infant has signs of circulation, tilt the head and give one breath every 3 seconds until the infant starts breathing again.

Check for signs of circulation occasionally while doing rescue breathing.

IF there are **no signs of circulation**, begin CPR:

1. Place the infant face up on a hard surface. Place 2 fingers on the breastbone one finger width below an imaginary line connecting the nipples.

2. Push down 1.2–2.5 cm (1/2–1 in) and release, 5 times every 3 seconds or less.

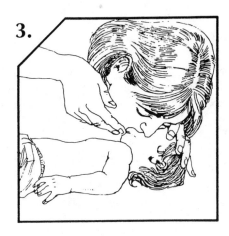

3. Tilt the head, cover the infant's mouth and nose with your mouth and give 1 slow puff.

4. Continue alternating cycles of 5 chest compressions and 1 puff.

49

Signs of circulation:
- responsiveness
- movement
- coughing
- effective breathing
- appropriate colour of skin
- presence of pulse (brachial)

5. Recheck for signs of circulation after about 1 minute of CPR.

If there are **no signs of circulation**, continue CPR, rechecking circulation and breathing every few minutes.

If there are signs of circulation, stop chest compressions. Continue blowing air in every 3 seconds until the infant starts breathing or EMS arrives.

☞ Red Cross Memory Aid:
A = airway
B = breathing
C = circulation

Breathing/CPR
Child 1 to 8 Years

IF the child does not respond to tapping or shouting,

Rescue Breathing Child

1. Shout for help and send someone to call EMS. If you are alone, "CALL FIRST."
2. Tilt the head to open the airway. Lift the chin with one hand and push down on the forehead with the other.
3. Check breathing for no more than 10 seconds. Place your cheek near the child's nose and mouth. Listen and feel for air. Look for movement of the chest.
4. If the child is breathing, care for **Unconsciousness**, page 95.

CAUTION: If you suspect a neck, head or back injury, do not tilt the head. Gently lift the chin without moving the neck or pressing on the forehead. Tilt the head only if you cannot inflate the chest.

2.

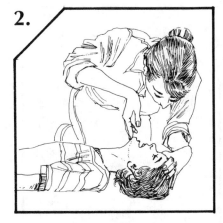

3.

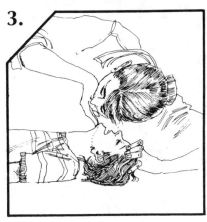

51

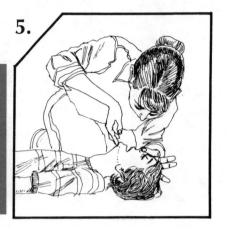

5.

6.

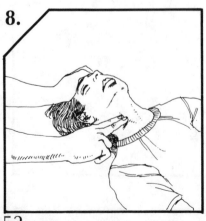

8.

5. If the child is **not breathing**, pinch the nostrils closed.

6. Seal your mouth around the child's mouth. Blow in two slow breaths of air. Look for movement of the chest.

7. **If the chest has not moved** after the first breath, make sure the head is tilted enough. Pinch the nostrils closed and try again. If the chest still does not move, turn to **Choking**, **Child**, page 64.

8. Check for **signs of circulation**. Look for movement, coughing, breathing, and appropriate colour of skin. Find the Adam's apple and slide your fingers into the groove at the side of the neck. Feel for a carotid pulse for no more than 10 seconds.

9. If the child has signs of circulation, tilt the head and give one breath every 3 seconds until the ambulance arrives, or until the child starts breathing again. Check for signs of circulation occasionally while doing Rescue Breathing.

IF there are **no signs of circulation**, begin CPR:

1. Gently tuck your hand under the child's far armpit and then slide your hand over the breastbone.

2. Use one hand. Keep the arm straight with elbow locked. Push down 2.5–3.8 cm (1–1½ in) and release, keeping your hand on the child's chest.

3. Push down and release 5 times in 3 seconds. Tilt the head and give 1 slow breath.

CAUTION: If the child vomits, roll him on his side, clean out the mouth and resume rescue breathing.

1.

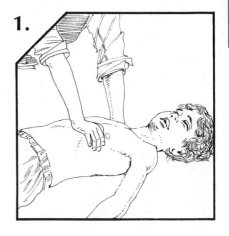

2.

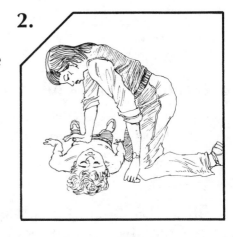

53

Signs of circulation:
- responsiveness
- movement
- coughing
- effective breathing
- appropriate colour of skin
- presence of pulse (carotid)

☞ Red Cross Memory Aid:

A = airway

B = breathing

C = circulation

4. Continue alternating cycles of 5 chest compressions and 1 breath.

5. After about 1 minute of CPR, recheck for signs of circulation.

If there are **no signs of circulation**, continue CPR, rechecking circulation and breathing every few minutes.

If there are signs of circulation, stop chest compressions. Continue with Rescue Breathing until the child starts breathing or EMS arrives.

Breathing/CPR—Child over 8 Years

Minor modifications are needed to perform Rescue Breathing or CPR on a child over 8 years old.

Rescue Breathing: Give larger breaths (1 breath every 5 seconds).

CPR: Use 2 hands at a rate of 15 chest compressions to 2 breaths (15:2). Press down 3.8–5 cm (1½–2 in).

Broken Bones

What to look for:

The presence of only one of these signs is sufficient to call an ambulance:

- severe pain or tenderness to the touch
- distortion of a limb
- loss of circulation in a limb (toes/fingers are white or blue)
- loss of feeling in a limb (Can the child feel a squeeze of the fingers or toes?)
- swelling and discoloration
- child reports having heard a cracking sound

What to do:

1. Immobilize the broken limb where the child is lying. Use towels or blankets to stabilize the limb.
2. Cool the area with wrapped ice for 15 minutes each hour.
3. Call an ambulance.
4. Comfort the child. Keep her warm.

CAUTION: Do not move a child who has a broken bone. Call an ambulance; the attendants will splint the bone.

NOTE:
The treatment for dislocations is the same as for broken bones.

1.

Broken Bones
With a Wound

What to do:

1. Gently place a cloth over the wound. Use a sterile dressing or clean cloth.

2. Apply slight pressure around but not on the wound without moving the broken bone.

3. Do not elevate the limb.

4. If bleeding is not controlled, apply a second bandage over the first.

5. Call an ambulance immediately.

6. Comfort the child. Keep him warm.

Burns
Chemical

Definition
◆ A chemical burn is an injury caused by exposure to chemicals, powder, liquid or gas.

What to do:

1. If the child is experiencing any difficulties with breathing or is unconscious, call an ambulance. Turn to **Breathing/CPR**, page 47 or **Unconsciousness**, page 95. For chemicals in the eyes, see page 71.

2. If not, identify the poison and call the Poison Control Centre for advice.

3. Flush the area with cool water.

4. Remove contaminated clothing unless the clothing is stuck to the skin. Continue to flush with water.

5. If no running water is available, gently brush off any dry chemicals, making sure that underlying skin is not damaged.

6. Comfort the child. Keep her warm.

CAUTION: Avoid spreading any of the poison on the patient or yourself.

3.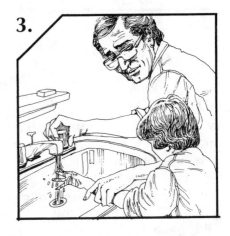

Burns
Heat

Definition

◆ Heat burns are caused by over-exposure to excessive heat; possible sources are fire, steam or sun.

CAUTION: Remove loose clothing around the affected area. Do not break blisters. Never use greasy ointments, butter, lotions or creams.

NOTE:
With all electrical burns, call for an ambulance and look for possible entry and exit burns that may need treatment. Carefully watch for breathing problems. See **Breathing/ CPR**, page 47.

What to do:

1. Immerse the burned area in cold water for at least 5 minutes or as long as the pain lasts. Do not use ice.

2. Cover the burn with a sterile, non-stick dressing.

3. Serious burns require immediate medical attention. These include red burns 5 cm (2") or more in diameter and all burns that are blistered, white or black. Call for an ambulance.

4. Comfort the child. Keep her warm.

Choking
Infant Under 1 Year

IF the infant can breathe or cough forcefully, do not interfere with her effort to free the object.

Do not hit the infant on the back. Stay with the infant and monitor closely.

IF the infant is:

- not breathing
- not coughing
- making a high-pitched noise, do the following:

Conscious Choking Infant

1. Place the infant face down on your hand and forearm with the head lower than the body, supporting her head firmly by holding the jaw. Rest your forearm on your thigh.

2. Deliver 5 sharp back blows between the shoulder blades. Use the heel of your hand. If this does not free the object,

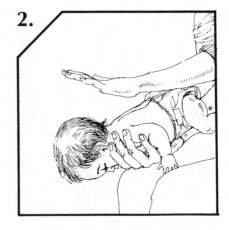

2.

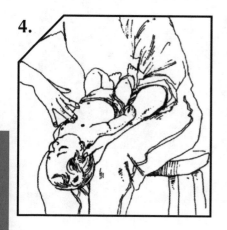

4.

3. Roll the infant face up with the head lower than the body. Support the head.

4. Place two fingers on the breast bone, one finger width below an imaginary line connecting the nipples.

5. Give 5 chest thrusts. Thrust approximately 1.2–2.5 cm ($^{1}/_{2}$–1 in).

6. Alternate back blows and chest thrusts until the object is dislodged.

7. Comfort the infant and keep her calm and warm. Have the infant checked by medical aid.

IF the infant becomes unconscious:

Unconscious Choking Infant

1. Shout for help and send someone to call EMS. If you are alone, "CALL FIRST."

2. Look in the mouth. Grasp the tongue and lower jaw. If you can see the object, remove it with your pinky finger.

3. Tilt the head to open the airway by placing your hand on the infant's forehead. With a finger of your other hand, lift the infant's chin. Check breathing for no more than 10 seconds.

4. If the infant is not breathing, seal your mouth over the infant's mouth and nose. Attempt to ventilate. Watch for movement of the chest.

2.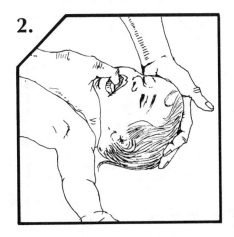

3.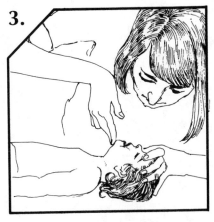

4.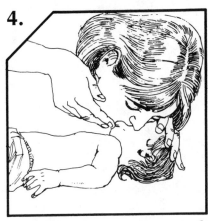

61

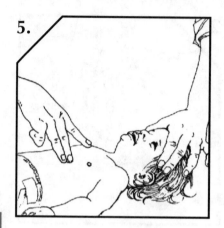

5.

If the air does not go in, reposition the head and reattempt the ventilation.

5. If the chest **does not rise**, start the CPR sequence (5 chest compressions).

6. Repeat the CPR sequence (5 chest compressions, look in the mouth, open the airway, and attempt to ventilate) until the airway is cleared. Remember, if necessary, to reposition the head to adjust the airway.

7. If the airway is cleared, but the infant is **not** breathing, continue to blow air in once every 3 seconds.

Turn to **Breathing/CPR**, page 47.

Choking
Child 1 to 8 Years

IF the child can breathe, speak or cough forcefully, encourage him to bend forward and cough up the foreign object.

Do not hit the child on the back. Stay with him and monitor closely.

IF the child is:

- not breathing, coughing or talking
- turning blue
- making a high-pitched noise, do the following:

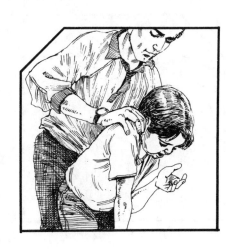

Conscious Choking Child

1. Stand behind the child and place your arms around his waist.

2. Make a tight fist. Place it just above the navel and well below the ribs, thumb against the abdomen. Place your other hand over this fist. Press your fist into the abdomen with quick upward thrusts.

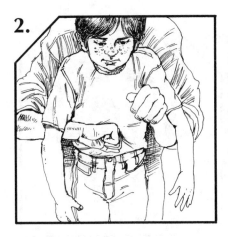

2.

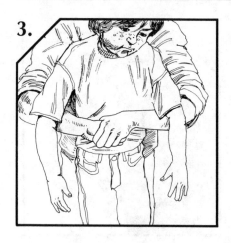

3. Continue the thrusts until the object has been expelled.

4. Comfort the child. Keep him calm and warm. Have the child checked by medical aid.

IF the child becomes unconscious:

Unconscious Choking Child

1. Call for help and send someone to call EMS. If you are alone, "CALL FIRST."

2. Look in the mouth. Grasp the tongue and lower jaw. If you can see the object, remove it, taking care not to push it further down the throat.

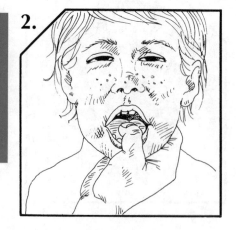

3. Tilt the head to open the airway. Lift the chin with one hand and push down on the forehead with the other. Check breathing for no more than 10 seconds.

4. If the child is not breathing, pinch the nostrils closed with the thumb and forefinger of the hand that is on the child's forehead.

5. Seal your mouth tightly around the child's mouth. Attempt to ventilate. Look for movement of the chest. If the air does not go in, reposition the head and reattempt the ventilation.

5.

6. If the chest **does not rise**, start the CPR sequence (5 chest compressions).

6.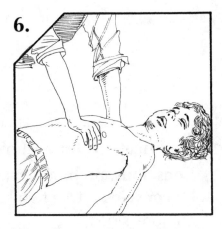

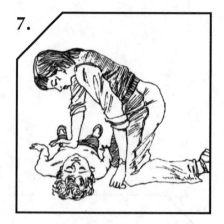

7. Repeat the CPR sequence (5 chest compressions, look in the mouth, open the airway, and attempt to ventilate) until the airway is cleared. Remember, if necessary, to reposition the head to adjust the airway.

8. If the child's airway is clear, **check for signs of circulation** for no more than 10 seconds. If there are no signs of circulation turn to **Breathing/CPR**, page 51.

9. If the child has **signs of circulation**, tilt the head and give one breath every 3 seconds until EMS arrives or the child starts breathing again.

Modifications for a Choking Child—Over 8 Years
Conscious: no modifications
Unconscious: Use two hands to perform 15 chest compressions

Cold
Frostbite

What to look for:
- area of skin whiter than the surrounding area
- pain or stinging followed by numbness
- most commonly affects noses, earlobes, fingers and toes

What to do:

Minor
1. Warm the area in your hands or under an armpit.
2. As the frostbitten area "thaws," the child will feel pain or a burning sensation.

CAUTION: Do not rub the frostbitten area or apply heat or snow.

Severe
1. Seek medical attention immediately for severe frostbite. Without medical care, fingers and toes may be badly damaged.
2. Remove any constrictive jewellery or clothing.

3.

3. Place the area in warm, not hot, 40.5°C (105°F) water until colour returns. Do not allow the limb to touch the sides of the bath.

4. Blisters may form. Do not break them. Protect them with a loose dressing.

5. Comfort the child. Keep her warm.

NOTE:

For a tongue stuck on metal in winter: warm the metal and tongue and carefully lift the tongue off the object. Never pull it off. Ensure the airway is kept clear.

Diabetes

What to look for:

- a child with history of diabetes who has taken too much insulin, missed a meal, or exercised excessively
- moist, ashen or pale skin
- cold sweat
- hunger
- shallow breathing
- confusion
- shaking
- dizziness
- aggressive behaviour
- uncharacteristic behaviour

What to do:

1. If the child is fully conscious, give him juice, honey or another food high in sugar.
2. Seek medical attention immediately.
3. Comfort the child. Keep him warm.

If the child is **Unconscious**, refer for page 95.

CAUTION: This condition may be life-threatening if not handled immediately.

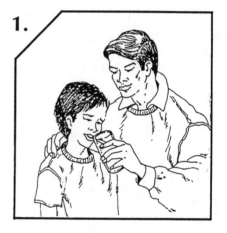

1.

NOTE:

The child may be carrying special sugar products that are quickly absorbed into the system. Ask the child if he has any and assist him to take them.

Electrical Shock

CAUTION: Do not touch the child until the power has been switched off.

What to do:

1. Shout for help and send someone for an ambulance.
2. **INDOORS:**
   Be sure the power is off by unplugging the appliance or switching off the breaker.
   OUTDOORS:
   Stay away from downed powerlines as they may electrify the ground.
3. Tap the child and ask, "Are you OK?" If no response, turn to **Unconsciousness**, page 96.
4. If the child is conscious, watch him closely.
5. Check for and treat burns, page 58.
6. Comfort the child. Keep him warm.

NOTE:

With all electrical burns, look for possible entry and exit injuries.

See **Breathing/CPR**, page 47.

Eyes
Chemical in the Eye

What to do:

1. Flush the eye thoroughly with lukewarm water for at least 15 minutes or as long as pain persists. Lift the upper and lower lids to totally expose the eye area.

2. Contact medical aid immediately.

3. Comfort the child. Keep him warm.

CAUTION: Wash the chemical away from the uninjured eye.

1.

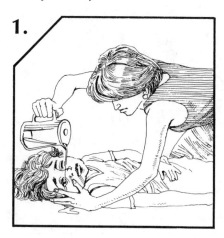

Eyes
Foreign Object in the Eye

What to do:

1. Instruct the child not to rub the injured eye.

2. Do not remove a foreign object that appears to adhere to or penetrate the eye in any way.

3. Cover the eye with a loose bandage to reduce eye movement. Avoid pressing the foreign object against the eye.

4. Call for an ambulance.

5. Comfort the child. Keep her warm.

NOTE:

Small loose particles may be removed by blinking or flushing with water. If the pain persists or the eye appears scratched, seek medical attention.

Fainting

Definition
◆ Fainting is a loss of consciousness due to temporary lack of blood flow to the brain.

What to look for:
Fainting may be preceded by:

- paleness
- sweating
- dizziness
- nausea

What to do:
1. If you think that the child is about to faint, have him lie down.

2. If the child does faint, place him in the recovery position and watch breathing and pulse closely.

3. As he awakens, keep him at rest and warm. Comfort him.

4. If the child does not rouse within a minute, treat for **Unconsciousness**, page 95.

2.

Fever

CAUTION: It is recommended that acetaminophen (e.g. Tylenol, Tempra, etc.) be used if you choose to give the child medication.

What to do:

1. To reduce a high fever, sponge the child with water at room temperature. Do not cause the child to shiver. Use medication for fever control.

2. Remove excess clothing and blankets. Give the child water, diluted juice or "flat" soft drinks.

NOTE:

A fever is the body's defense mechanism at work. A mild fever should not be a concern unless it continues for more than three days. If the child's temperature rises to 39°C (102°F) or if it is not easily controlled, seek medical attention.

Head Injuries

What to look for:

- headache
- dizziness or disorientation
- nausea or vomiting
- drowsiness or loss of consciousness
- bleeding or fluid from the ears or nose
- unequal pupils or failure of the eyes to move together
- convulsions
- difficulty in moving or using limbs
- lumps or bumps on the head

What to do:

1. Check for consciousness. Ask, "Are you O.K.?"

2. If the child is conscious and you suspect a neck injury, immobilize the head in the position found. Use whatever is available to support the child in place.

CAUTION: A child that has received a head injury must receive medical attention and be watched carefully for 24 hours.

CAUTION: Any head injury may mean the child also has a neck or back injury. Unless the child's life is in danger, do not move her.

2.

3. Call an ambulance.
4. If the child is bleeding, cover the wound with a dressing and apply direct pressure.
5. Tape or bandage the dressing in place.
6. Comfort the child. Keep her warm.
7. If the child is unconscious, shout for help and send someone for an ambulance. Refer to **Unconsciousness**, page 95.

NOTE:

A fall of 15 cm (6") onto a hard surface is sufficient to cause a head injury. Seek medical attention immediately. A head injury may be more severe than it seems.

Heat Exhaustion

Definition

◆ Heat exhaustion is an excessive demand on the body to cool itself.

What to look for:

- cool, moist, pale or red skin
- headache
- exhaustion
- weakness and dizziness
- nausea and vomiting

What to do:

1. Move the child to a cool, shady area.
2. Comfort her.
3. Replace lost fluids by giving sips of water.
4. Gradually cool the child by removing excess clothing and fanning her constantly. If she starts shivering, stop fanning.

CAUTION: If the child's temperature rises, and if her perspiration stops, refer to **Heatstroke**, page 78.

3.

Heatstroke

Sunstroke

Definition

◆ Heatstroke is an advanced form of **Heat Exhaustion.** The body has lost its ability to cool itself.

What to look for:

- hot, dry, reddish skin
- no sweating
- high temperature (39°C, 102°F)
- headache, nausea, vomiting

What to do:

CAUTION: Heatstroke is life-threatening. If it is advanced, the child may lose consciousness.

1. Move the child to a cool, shady place.
2. Call for an ambulance.
3. Bathe the child as quickly as possible with large amounts of cool water, or wrap him in wet, cold sheets. Concentrate on cooling the head, armpits, groin.
4. If the child is conscious and not feeling nauseated, give him sips of water.
5. Comfort the child.
6. If the child becomes **Unconscious**, turn to page 95.

Hyperventilation

Definition

◆ Hyperventilation is an imbalance in the body's natural breathing process often triggered by an upsetting situation.

What to look for:

• uncontrolled gasping for air
• dizziness
• panic
• anxiety

What to do:

1. Comfort the child. Encourage her to take long, slow breaths and to hold her breath before breathing out slowly.

2. If the child faints, care for **Fainting**, page 73.

CAUTION: Make sure any medical condition or injury has been ruled out.

Hypothermia
Mild

Definition

◆ Hypothermia is a dangerous lowering of inner body temperature that may occur when a child is exposed to cold air, cool wind, wet clothing or prolonged immersion in water.

What to look for:

- complaints of feeling cold
- shivering
- irritable
- uncharacteristic clumsiness

What to do:

1. Replace wet clothing with dry clothes and blankets.
2. Cover the head and neck.
3. If the child is fully conscious and can swallow, give him a warm, sweet, non-alcoholic liquid.
4. Apply warmth such as hot water bottles to the armpits and groin, avoiding direct contact with the skin.

1.

NOTE:

Alcohol increases heat loss and should never be given to a person suffering from hypothermia.

Hypothermia
Severe

What to look for:
- lack of coordination
- fumbling hands
- slurred speech
- memory lapse
- blurred vision
- shivering stops
- muscles become stiff
- unconsciousness

Infants may show the following signs:
- mottled cheeks and limbs
- no crying
- weak sucking

What to do:
1. Call an ambulance immediately.
2. Place the child in a warm, dry place.
3. Do not allow the child to move around. Treat the child very gently.
4. Replace all wet clothing with dry clothes and blankets. Prevent further heat loss.

5. Monitor the child's breathing and circulation.

6. If the child becomes **Unconscious**, refer to page 95.

NOTE:
Alcohol increases heat loss and should never be given to a person suffering from hypothermia.

Infection

Definition

◆ Infection is contamination from dirt, foreign bodies or bacteria present in a wound which the body's own immune system has been unable to destroy.

What to look for:

- swelling, redness and warmth around the wound
- pain in the area of the wound
- possible pus discharge

More serious infection may cause:

- fever, feeling ill
- red streaks that progress from the wound towards the heart

CAUTION: If fever or red streaks are present, seek medical attention immediately.

What to do:

1. Keep the wound clean and dry.
2. Cover with a sterile dressing.
3. Seek medical attention.

NOTE:

Prevention is the best defense against infection. Ensure that all wounds are cleaned and bandaged properly.

Confirm with your doctor that immunizations are up to date. Infants should receive their first inoculation, which includes tetanus, at approximately 2 months. A tetanus booster is recommended every 5 to 10 years.

Moving the Injured Child

What to look for:

- immediate danger to the child or rescuer that cannot be removed

What to do:

CAUTION: Do not move an injured child who may have a head, back or neck injury unless the child is in danger where he is. Only move the child if you cannot eliminate the danger.

1. If you have only a few seconds to rescue a child, dragging may be necessary. Cradle the head in your forearms to protect it. Drag the child by the shoulders or clothing.

2. If you suspect a neck or back injury, but must move the child, prevent head and neck movement as much as possible.

Neck and Back

What to look for:

One or more of the following:

- loss of motion or sensation below the injury
- pain at site of injury
- light muscle flinching
- "pins and needles" sensation below the site of the injury
- confusion
- loss of co-ordination

CAUTION: Unless the child's life is in danger, do not move him.

What to do:

1. Shout for help and send someone for an ambulance.

2. Check for consciousness without moving the child. Ask "Are you O.K.?"

3. If conscious, immobilize the head and body in the position found. Use whatever is available.

4. If **Unconscious**, turn to page 95.

5. Comfort the child. Keep him warm.

3.

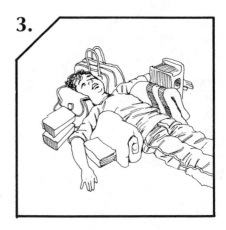

Poisons
Swallowed

What to look for:

If a chemical has been swallowed:

- burning sensation in the mouth, throat or stomach
- cramps, gagging, diarrhoea
- unconsciousness

If a plant or drug has been swallowed:

- vomiting, convulsions
- irregular pulse
- drowsiness, slurred speech, dizziness, lack of co-ordination

What to do:

1. If the child is experiencing any difficulties with breathing or is unconscious, call an ambulance. Turn to **Breathing/CPR**, page 47, or **Unconsciousness**, page 95.

2. If not, identify the poison and call the Poison Control Centre for advice.

CAUTION: Never attempt to make an unconscious child vomit.

3. Send a sample of the poison and any vomit with the child to the hospital.

4. Comfort him and keep him warm.

Poisons
Inhaled

What to look for:

- irritated eyes, nose or throat
- coughing, shortness of breath, dizziness
- vomiting, convulsions
- bluish colour around the mouth
- unconsciousness

What to do:

1. Protect yourself from the gases. Ensure the air is safe. (The child may have to be moved.)
2. If the child is experiencing any difficulties with breathing or is unconscious, call an ambulance. Turn to **Breathing/CPR**, page 47, or **Unconsciousness**, page 95.
3. If not, call the Poison Control Centre for advice.
4. Comfort the child. Keep her warm.

Poisons
On the Skin

What to look for:

- burning, itching, swelling, blisters
- headache, fever

What to do:

1. If the child is experiencing any difficulties with breathing or is unconscious, call an ambulance. Turn to **Breathing/CPR**, page 47, or **Unconsciousness**, page 95.

2. If not, identify the poison and call the Poison Control Centre for advice.

3. If a rash develops, apply a paste of baking soda and water to the area several times a day. Lotions such as Calamine® or Caladryl® may be soothing.

4. If lesions or blisters develop or the rash persists, seek medical attention.

5. Comfort the child. Keep him warm.

NOTE:
For chemicals on the skin, see **Burns, Chemical**, page 57.

Seizures / Convulsions

Definition
◆ Seizures are severe, uncontrolled muscle spasms.

What to do:
1. Shout for help and send someone for an ambulance.

2. Protect the child's head and limbs from injury by removing nearby objects. Place pillows or other soft objects between the child's head and immovable objects such as walls and heavy furniture.

3. Do not interfere with the child's movements.

4. Do not put objects between the teeth or in the mouth.

5. After the seizure, place the child in the recovery position.

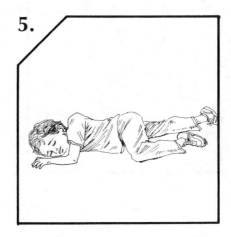

6. Comfort the child. Keep him warm.

7. If the child is unconscious, turn to **Unconsciousness**, page 95.

Slivers

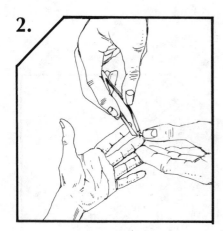

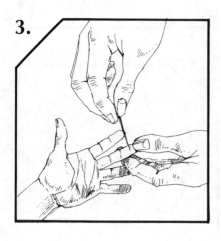

What to do:

1. Wash the area around the sliver.

2. If the sliver is sticking out of the skin, use tweezers to pull it out. Pull in the same angle and direction that the sliver entered the skin.

3. If the sliver is embedded under the skin, use a needle to remove it. With the needle, gently pull the skin away from around the sliver where it entered the skin. Remove it with tweezers.

4. Wash the area with soap and water. Cover the wound with a bandage.

NOTE:

If the skin around the cut becomes infected (red and sore to the touch), seek medical attention.

Sprains and Strains

Definition

◆ A **sprain** is an injury to a joint. A **strain** is an injury caused by overstretching the muscles.

What to look for:

- swelling
- pain
- discoloration
- loss of movement

What to do:

1. Place the child in a comfortable position. If you suspect a sprain, do not move the child unless necessary. The injury could involve a broken bone.

2. Apply cold to the injured area. Do not allow ice to touch the skin. Wrap the ice in a towel or cloth and apply for 15 minutes every hour.

3. Seek medical attention.

4. Comfort the child. Keep her warm.

2.

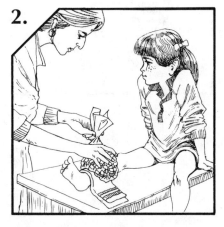

☞ Red Cross Memory Aid:

R = rest

I = immobilize

C = cold

E = elevate

93

Teeth

What to look for:
- history of blow to mouth
- wound to mouth area
- chipped or broken teeth

What to do:
1. Tilt the child's head forward to prevent choking on blood.
2. Apply direct pressure to the mouth wounds. Use a piece of gauze or clean cloth over the socket. Have the child bite down to hold the dressing in place.

3. Collect knocked-out teeth. Place them in cool water or milk.
4. Seek **dental** attention immediately to have the teeth re-implanted.
5. Comfort the child. Keep her warm.

NOTE:
Blood and loose teeth may obstruct the airway. Watch closely.

Unconsciousness

What to do:

1. Tap the child and ask, "Are you O.K.?" If there is no response, shout for help and send someone to call an ambulance.

2. If the child is breathing, place the child in the recovery position.

   Turn the body as a unit. Avoid twisting the neck. Ask other adults to assist you. Keep the mouth clear of blood and vomit.

3. Constantly check breathing. If the child is **not** breathing, turn to **Breathing/CPR**, page 47.

4. Comfort the child. Keep her warm.

CAUTION: If a neck or back injury is suspected, be very careful to keep the neck from moving.

2.

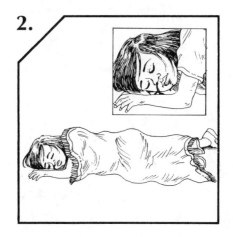

First Aid Supplies

A first aid kit should contain the following:

1. Emergency telephone numbers for EMS, the poison control centre, and personal physicians. Include the home and office phone numbers of family members, friends, or neighbours who can help.
2. Sterile gauze pads (dressings), in small and large squares to place over wounds.
3. Adhesive tape.
4. Roller and triangular bandages to hold dressings in place or to make an arm sling.
5. Adhesive bandages in assorted sizes.
6. Scissors.
7. Tweezers.
8. Safety pins.
9. Ice bag or chemical ice pack.
10. Disposable gloves such as surgical or examination gloves.
11. Flashlight, with extra batteries in a separate bag.
12. Antiseptic wipes or soap.
13. Pencil and pad.
14. Emergency blanket.
15. Eye patches.
16. Thermometer.
17. Barrier devices (i.e., pocket mask or face shield).
18. Coins for a pay phone.
19. Canadian Red Cross First Aid manual.

NOTE:

A **dressing** is the material placed on the wound. It may be a clean cloth, sterile gauze or a commercial non-stick product.

A **bandage** holds a dressing in place. It may be cloth or adhesive tape.

A **wound dressing** is a commercial product that had a thick absorbent dressing attached to a bandage.

Personal
Emergency Information

Child's Name _____

Date of Birth _____

Parent or Guardian's Name & Address _____

_____

	Name	Telephone
Paediatrician	_____	_____
Family Physician	_____	_____
Specialist	_____	_____
Dentist	_____	_____

MEDICAL INSURANCE

Policy Number _____

Company Phone Number _____

ALLERGIES

_____   _____

_____   _____

CHRONIC CONDITIONS

_____   _____

_____   _____

SPECIAL INFORMATION AND PRECAUTIONS

_____

First Aid Index

Take a Look at All the Other Ways Red Cross Can Serve You

First Aid Courses

Our Standard and Emergency First Aid and CPR courses provide you with the skills necessary to respond to any emergency – from broken bones to bleeding and from head injuries to heart attacks.

PeopleSavers Program

Be sure your child knows what to do in an emergency. Enroll them in the PeopleSavers Program: a first aid and safety program for children ages 5-12.

Babysitter's Course

Has your sitter taken the Red Cross Babysitter's course? This course teaches adolescents to care for your children, how to do basic first aid and how to keep the children's environment safe.

Water Safety

You can never be too careful around water. Have your children taken swimming lessons? Are they familiar with water safety? Enroll in Canada's biggest and best Water Safety course. Call us – or your local pool.

First Aid Kits

Make sure you are prepared for emergencies in your home. Do you have a first aid kit? A variety of kits are available from your local Red Cross. Make sure you have a kit in your home and your car!

IT FEELS GOOD TO KNOW YOU HAVE HELPED
BE A FINANCIAL DONOR – Please give, we do!

The Canadian Red Cross Society offers many other courses and services.

For more information, contact your local Red Cross office.